Romanticism

Romanticism

poems

APRIL BERNARD

W. W. NORTON & COMPANY   NEW YORK   •   LONDON

For information about permission to reproduce selections from this book,
write to Permissions, W. W. Norton & Company, Inc.,
500 Fifth Avenue, New York, NY 10110

For information about special discounts for bulk purchases, please contact
W. W. Norton Special Sales at specialsales@wwnorton.com or 800-233-4830

Manufacturing by Courier Westford
Book design by Chris Welch
Production manager: Julia Druskin

Library of Congress Cataloging-in-Publication Data

Bernard, April.
Romanticism : poems / April Bernard. — 1st ed.
p. cm.
ISBN 978-0-393-06807-8
I. Title.
PS3552.E7258R66 2009
811'.54—dc22

2009005631

W. W. Norton & Company, Inc.
500 Fifth Avenue, New York, N.Y. 10110
www.wwnorton.com

W. W. Norton & Company Ltd.
Castle House, 75/76 Wells Street, London W1T 3QT

1 2 3 4 5 6 7 8 9 0

to my mother and father

Contents

II.

III.

Romanticism

I

The Going

The cloth edge of certainty
has shredded down to this:
God and love are real,
but very far away.
If I go to Istanbul, will I return?
That is not one of the permitted questions.
When I go to Istanbul, how will I bear to return?
I could slip into the small streets
that lead away from the souk, then run east
to the high plain and the Caucasus—

It's all alone, the returning,
the going. The cloth,
a soft holland whose blocks of blue and lemon
once cheered me in a skirt,
now dries dishes. God and love
are very far away, farther even
than the mountains in the east.

The Paper Goose

is sticky-winged, the beast of my sorrow
oiled by fear coming off my fingertips,
working the dull folds to stiffen and blot.

The beast of my sorrow crumples and wads;
it will not unfold into fluttering pennant, flowing water.
Instead, all recalcitrance, it sinks as sorrow.

Greedy Thing,

we called the dingo bitch who hung around the camp,
mustard brown with black streaks and filmy eyes.
At night she ate the chickens, feet and heads.

Her ruff rose spiky when she menaced the children
until they gave her their sandwiches. We threw stones,
which she always licked, once or twice, in case.

A Chthonic Deity

drags behind her a cloud sack,
grey and purple, which leaks perpetually
and never empties: She wishes to go

aloft, but she is not a sky-god,
she is of the earth and her name cannot be spoken
through the choke of rain.

Beagle or Something

The composer's name was Beagle or something,
one of those Brits who make the world wistful
with chorales and canticles and this piece,
a tone poem or what-have-you,
chimes and strings aswirl, dangerous for one
whose eye lids and sockets have been rashing from tears.
The music occupied the car where
I had parked and then sat, staring at
a tree, a smallish maple,
fire-gold and half-undone by the wind,
shaking in itself,
shocking blue morning sky behind, and also
the trucks and telephone wires and dogs
and children late to school along Orange Street, but
it was the tree that caused an uproar,
it was the tree that shook and shed,
aureate as a shaken soul, I remembered
I was supposed to have one—for convenience

I placed it in my chest, the heart being away,
and now it seems the soul has lodged there, shaking,
golden-orange, half-spent but clanging
truer than Beagle music or my forehead pressed
hard on the steering wheel in petition for release.

Waking Alone

is sad and valuable instruction. It happens often
in the night, as my chow-dog's ghost
still performs her sentry patrols:

Every hour or so, snorting herself awake
to visit another doorway, falling again into snores,
blocking all means by which a stranger might come.

Pull the Water Lily

up by its long snake stem
into the boat. And more: Dozens of lilies,
armloads of twining stems,

a wet haul white and gold and green.
Again the boat pushes into the weeds.
I have asked for more than water to drink.

Renunciation

takes time. Since life is even more finely calibrated
than a Henry James story, I find I must
resolve to lose repeatedly

yet not believe myself.
"Satan and all his works" is easy; but
there are no rites to assist me here.

Straw Flowers

arrive as good as dead, yet surely
white roots once wetly fingered soil, green stem began
with flexible waist. What mistakes arise

from the hint of water: In Sonora, after one rain,
a bean seed disrobed to greenish flesh,
before the gesture arrested at drought.

To the Knife

I think I hate Ben Hecht, or Hitchcock, or myself
for surely we are the ones who made those lovers dance
badly, fiercely, in *Notorious*, where I discovered myself

a long time ago, before I learned the finish of the dance
could never be a box-office-pleasing slow dissolve to kissing.
No; my dance like theirs properly never ends, it is a *danse*

apache to the death, so much violence to reason in lovers kissing
and sighing, because they love because it's impossible,
and pretending a happy ending is just an excuse for more kissing.

My mouth, his mouth, to the Brazilian sway and bite of impossibly
tender jaws, jewels and fingernails incising the shadows intimate
with jacaranda and the darker smells, we lovers who believe love possible

as a temporary proposition only; who can be intimate
with the flesh, we ask, when we are already intimate with death?
Flesh deliquesces, first with desire, then with death. I can't intimate

to another even by words where my passions knife-
skate on the edge of death, cool on the checkered floor of dissolution.
Not being able to love for long—now that's the knife

to run your fingertip along, as maracas shakey-shake; here's a solution
to every "fat-headed guy full of pain" who never
would say, "I'm a fat-headed guy full of pain," a dissolution

of dolce de leche to bile noir on the tongue of my own ever-
loving self. When I say it's "all a lot of hooey,"
I mean forgive me. I mean it's doomed for never.

Literature and the lesser candy-land arts filled me with that hooey
to which a daddy's girl succumbs forever more:
The love like a slap, the slap called love, the furious refusal: Hooey.

Did you know that Cary Grant loved me even more
than he loved Ingrid Bergman? His eyes, black vortices in the samba night,
found me there, in my dark, and promised me nothing more.

In a Stolen Boat,

push off what seemed safe: The fishing dock,
pitch pines, children glazed to sheen
by ruthless summers. Past

the jetty, past the past, to open sea—
all violet and green, that choppy path between doom and luck—
Put your back into it, and row.

II

The Heroine in the Novel

Early Days

Rucked-up knickers, standing in the pond
with a cheesecloth net. Frogs and the golden Japanese carp
she caught from the stock the groundsmen had added
that spring. And she fed them to her snake.
(She is Abigail, her novel is *Under the Rose*
by Langley Boisvert, published in London in 1886.)
Hair-tossing was a habit, and ringlets
pulled back under a blue straw bonnet. Oh, and that laugh,
a *merry* laugh it was, and her eyes often
danced, I am afraid. But
she had a chin like a prize fighter.

Out and About

Three soldiers committed suicide in her first season
when she turned them down. It was remarked that two
were captains, one a colonel. Rank, of course,
meant nothing to her. After she jilted the son of an earl,
the scandal sheet demanded: "Lady or Tiger?"
She found that unbecoming
and, briefly, trimmed her claws to the nub.
What they could not know, she too was unable to know,
the nature of herself being unknowable to her nature, veiled, that is,
woman who is not known and will not be known until it is too late
and still she will not be seen, she will be unknowable
and even when she looks in the mirror
she sees not a thing. Except those ringlets,
glossy chestnut ringlets.

Settled

Abigail acquired banker husband, then boy, then twin girls, and full
household staff. The cares of ceaselessly
apportioned foods and drinks. The occasional *frisson*
of rucked-down knickers in the conservatory, muffled
giggles from the old row-boat. The stars and a sort
of domestic helium carried her through
the faceted vertiginous glare of dinner, through salmon russe
and those silly young men, the hobbledehoys
who needed a firm hand. She was said
to be quick-witted but unquotable, with a voice like sun melting
morning hoarfrost. A scent, chiefly citrus and ambergris,
was mixed in Paris for her exclusive use,
and it was known that she herself directed the terms
of the new trade treaty with Austro-Hungary.

Indiscreet

And yet it got out of hand. She was misled
into thinking this one safe because he was, of all things,
tow-headed. It was not accessible
to her imagination that sun-spreckled skin
and mild grey eyes would exact a payment, and from *her*.
The unravelling of her garments ensued: The small house
in Islington where she was exiled with her girls while her son
was sent away and her husband continued to make money
but with the aid of other female hands. The stock swindle—
that, at least, was not on her watch.
Rumor had it that she would not age gracefully,
and rumor had it wrong.

Last Glimpse

See her rummage through her escritoire.
That trinket of bulbous Baja pearl,
hanging from a coin-purse latch, a gift from her dear Mama.
The letters sheaved in a lavender ribbon (the ribbon edged
with tiny loops of silk) that catches on a fingernail.
She has been known to know a few things, lately,
and she knows this, as she fiddles with the rings
on her still-slim fingers: She knows
that no harm she has done comes close
to what has stabbed at her, what now stabs—
these cheap losses. The Chinese yellow
of her day-gown flatters her skin to a peach glow,
which helps a good deal. She puts the letters back
in the drawer, the ribbon rent but not untied.

All Right Already,

it doesn't change any more than that vine, you tear it off
and burn it up, there's sting in the smoke but it's back
in the spring. Call in the experts,

it can't be done. It shags the trees gaudy in this country
and trails you with its glossy pricks, sweet
velvet and unsleeping shade.

Roy Orbison and John Milton
Are Still Dreaming

You know what I mean: In the instant
of waking in bliss, the whole body smiles—

He's still alive—She came back—They didn't mean it—
We forgive and are forgiven—It all turned out—

And then the hand claws the duvet,
seized by the real, as all that's warm just drops.

I know you know. But I seek a potion
to make me dream of the actual with the same fervor,

so I'll wake to happy facts: It's spring! It's raining! Robins!
Someone will return a phone call today! My son

has watched the clock and let me nap for 35 minutes!—
and does not notice my face smacked wet

by the snap of the delusion, unmatched in sweetness,
that you promised to hold me always.

The Oft-Wedded Waif

homage to Edward Gorey

As an infant, Clothilde Hornbeam was wrapped in a kerchief and left in a thicket.

She was adopted by wolves.

Eventually, they banished her.

She was taken in by the nuns at the Convent of the Impenetrable Heart.

She learned to play the organ, and wrote liturgical music in a secret language.

"Burn me in the fire and eat my fingers off / Babies are tasty, so don't get in the way," she sang.

An incident in the potting shed made it plain she lacked a vocation.

Clothilde's first husband lost his nose in a fracas.

Her second husband ran away to join a pirate crew.

He sent home a macaw, who said: "I'm sorry, I'm sorry, I'm sorry."

While married to her third husband, a race-track tout, Clothilde opened a bakery.

Cookies in the shape of babies and wolf cubs were her specialty.

After her fourth and fifth husbands were apprehended by the authorities, Clothilde could be found weeping into the icing.

The tear-dripped cookies secured her fortune.

Concerning Romanticism
Early and late, its perils and pleasures,
in various lights

War

Today, as I rub my nose itching from wood smoke, I see
a specific water drop, droobling over the gutter
and, helpless, plopping to the ground. It destroys
the smooth surface of the snow, a wet knife boring in.
Thereby we may claim a moral, of the individual's power
                                    to annihilate the whole.

Or, dear heart, re-read the text that nature spells and see
the water as all one, no matter the form or temperature,
slush or crystal or soft dew drop. Again re-read; and see
the unified force of rain, the army of water
spilling from the sky and the gutters upon one lonely patch
                                    of yesterday's snow.

In the photo from 1917, the Russian soldiers are centaurs,
massive in formation, marching with high steps to the path
through the wood. Mist rises from the snow, as
the commander with the tall hat raises his arm towards
a lowering sky, from which snow descends. He can read
the sky and snow, as can we.

Let's take red ink from the bottle on the desk and drip it
over the photo's exquisite whites and blacks. Here
the emblems of color will accomplish the effect, or,
better, tear the photo to small confetti, toss
the handful from the window and make a parade
on the damaged snow.

How many have pushed their faces close to the dying,
hoping to smell out the secret that will explain
our slaughter to ourselves? We must crave it,
though we sorrow for it, caressing the gun and its partner bayonet.
I am searching you for the scent now. Give me my freedom
and you may kill me for it.

Manners

Is a blue grosgrain ribbon on a pale purple beaver felt fedora
more romantic than that ribbon tied loose about the throat?

Is Herr Professor adjusting his glasses
more exciting than the Cossack taking off his boots?

No; and no.

Something could be said for the putting *on*
of glasses and boots and hats—

But what? Enthusiasts for such can only be those who prefer
enlightenment, clear sight, the civilized pleasures of garb and more garb.

Such as they, who inhabit an age of reason,
may do just as well with an automated fuck;

but Oh not I.

Picture Postcard

Diesel smell, and the cluck-cluck-cluck of the vaporetto engine,
before the pilot slams it against the dock. Eccolo:

Whereas the gondoliers are marvels of graceful exactness
who never scratch their black swans, their cousins

the vaporetto pilots are perfect clods. Thunk, another chunk torn
    from
the dock, coming and going the same thunks.

Where is Ruskin? His palazzo's back, a chalky sunrise pink,
snubs the canal, and there is no finding the front door.

Henry James is swimming under the Rialto Bridge,
his corpus magically unharmed by the wash of the chemical lagoon.

Byron, drunk on chocolate, sucks on Mary Shelley's satin shoe
under a table at Florian's.

The pearly sky shrugs eternal shoulders and laughs,
or weeps, it is impossible to tell which.

Romance

I pine. There is an obstacle to our love.

Every time I hear the postman, I think: At last, the letter!
He has overcome the obstacle—

(It is a large obstacle, an actual alp, with a tree line and sheer rock face
streaked with snow even in July)

for love of me! For three years, nine decades, and one century or so, there
has been no letter. I still wait for the letter.

But lately I wonder if my predicament is outside the human,
neither noble nor farcical; if my heart courts pain

because it aims for immortality, something grander
than I can imagine. Most of what I imagine,

what I want, is small: Hands with mine in the sink, washing dishes,
the smell of wool, feet tangling mine in bed. I know

the gods punish the proud, but I do not yet know
why they punish the humble. Although after all

it is not humble to ask, every minute or so, for happiness.

Heart or Head Canard

Division of some sort prevails at all times. Take longing, soul,
gut, mind, impulse, intuition, belief, heart, head, logic—
and these just within, and each endlessly divisible. My old soul
fights my new soul that fights
the soul about to be born. Exteriorly there's advice, suggestion,
expert opinion, sounding board, law, custom, morality,
commandments, adages, fortune cookies, tarot readings,
weather forecasts, and bad news over the phone.

Some days it would be easier to find a steeple to climb,
with a nice old big old bell, and stand up under it,
and let the clapper bang and the bell swoop and knock and
—aside from extensive injuries—that would be an easier way
to start the day, in a clamor of brass and skin.
Descend the ladder after that Matins and walk forth.

Limit

His face opens and you see the sun.

(Peonies, fizzy wine, fanfares, gongs.)

You would do anything for him;

you scarcely think of yourself.

But you will not die for him.

The boundless thing, Romance,

known for the first time, and at once

its limit. Or yours: *You will not die.*

Underneath

Once you could have found my body in a partly opened grave, in the sands that blow and resettle at the foot of a ruined city. Gilt peels like sunburn from the plaster there.

Later on I tried to sit up and a beast, head of a goat and torso of a man but with stumpy chicken legs and wings, sat on my chest and smothered my face with damp insinuations and a smell like days-dead flesh.

Once I was under a cloud.

Do you know what it means to be "under erasure," that lovely post-structural notion, your words and deeds red-lined-through by some revisionist, who may be guiding your hand so that you are complicit in the silencing?

Under snow I have also been, snow that fell cleanly. When I was under snow it took a lot to persuade me to dig out, and now and then I think of that ice burrow with real longing.

At last I found this Norman church, in rubble of course. Beneath its broken wishbone ribs, amongst its heaps of plinths and flags, where the wind-knocked pines and the holm oak over steady centuries grow—here I sit, on the moss that pads the stones. The sounds of a nearby stream, calls of the red hawk, brief gusts through the branches, all cheer me.

Hush, now. I am trying to think.

Corollary

Just as the whelk-shell, so I have spiraled.

That's not it.

As the ibis feeds, so I have fed, and fed.

As the barley breathes gold-green in the wind, so I—

Let me say this plain:

I loved one as nothing else.

As the calyx anchors, then looses, the petals of the rose.

III

Paler Hands

in memory of Agha Shahid Ali

A garden filled with jasmine, oranges, moss—
here's perfume to invoke it, kid, tonight.

If you don't want me to spit like Bette's Jezebel,
don't jut your chin like Heston as El Cid tonight.

When told that ghazal rhymes with muzzle, my failure
is embodied, pillared in a mute caryatid tonight.

Cedar chips touched by flame, the scent
will always remind us what we didn't, and did, tonight.

You teased but somehow knew to name my fear:
"All alone in America." Heaven forbid tonight.

The puzzle of the ghazal like alien stars
makes awkward constellations on the grid tonight.

Agha, always "your highness," I the lowly spring
pour April libations on your parted lips, Shahid, tonight.

Flute

Some say *Here,*
it goes here, in a tin
on the shelf.
But others carry feeling
in the blood,
they say *Here,*
put your mouth
here, offering
the opulence
of a honeyed ear,
peppery mouths,
all the days
of a life. If
I weary of
gorgeous
kashmiri airs
fluting
through me,
nonetheless
these are
invitations

I am powerless
to hush. I was born
an open
reed
and not all
the sad lessons
so freely given—
today it was
the hurt, again—
can stop it

Bouncy Ballad

Yon hieland bonny, hieland lassie,

strides across the brae.

She beckons aye to horse and doggie,

she has laughter for herself and all.

Within her bides the one she loved,

the clown who capered aboard the ship

as it sailed forever and gone.

Ships that sail past Greenland way,

those ships do not return.

Fare thee well, my bonny laddie,

I've saved up the love in your eyes.

Buttermilk froth and strawberry jam,

knife for the bread on the scrubbed pine board,

there's a feast to feed my friends.

Sonya to the Messenger

aria from Claude DuFarge's The Cossack's Bride

I have written a message of love,
suitable for Saint Valentine's Day,
but I have disguised my handwriting
and it is unsigned—
Alas, he despises my name.

Please take this sealed to the village in the south,
ask for the blacksmith,
see that he receives this note,
but swear you do not know who sent it—
Alas, he will never forgive me.

May the light love words make him smile,
may he think of a pretty girl in the market
or some milkmaid he likes to watch
as she swings down the lane with her bucket yoke—
Alas, he despises my name.

Will you make sure the ruffians
at the tavern do not rob him
when he gets so drunk he can't walk?
Will you see him safe home to his wife?
Alas, he will never forgive me.

Please, with these extra coins,
buy him a sheepskin hat.
See for me if his eyes are still soft,
his cheeks smudged with soot from his forge.
Never, never, say my name.

Epithalamion

duet from The Cossack's Bride

Flame of my candle, yet burn!
Hand on my breast, I kiss you!
In the sweet moments of waking,
I am a bird at last in her proper nest.

A warm scent rises from my bridegroom
like mist from the river.
How my beloved's hand pinions my hair
as he sleeps, his other hand upon my breast!

Torrents and fire-storms of night
were but prelude to this sweet calm;
tumult has loosed its own ropes,
the bite has softened to the kiss.

Heimatlos

aria from Annalissa Beagle's The Ice God

Don't ask me if I have a home
unless you want to see the fjord open across my face,
the water that cuts into the land as if looking
for a place to cease and be safe
from tides.

Don't ask me if I have a home
if you can't bear to hear
of the years of wandering, the false starts,
the tender song that shuddered with the knowledge
of the second verse's sigh.

And don't ask me if I have a home
unless you've seen the place
for me, a kitchen window
where the sun sits, and a plate
of yellow and blue.

Don't ask me if I have a home
because the homeless veer like a flock across a field,
panicked sideways at the failing light that sends them
southward, to the end
of seasons.

Mary Star of the Morning

from The Ice God

[*Chorus of the Mothers enters, singing*]

The hand you raised in tender surprise
When the angel announced your fate
The same hand that curled round your baby's head
To bring him to your breast

O Mary Star of the Morning
Lift that hand to bless our task
We are your children, behold our babies
We march with torches and picks

[*Chorus of the Children enters, singing*]

Mary, bless our mothers
Give each the strength of a thousand mothers

[*Chorus of the Mothers*]

In your tender countenance
We find courage to march and sing
We praise and thank your watchfulness
We march in the light of your eyes

O Mary Star of the Morning,
See we have smashed the Ice God tonight
Join us at the river that hurries down the rocks
At the deep pool laugh and drink with us

[*Chorus of the Children*]

Mary, bless our mothers
Give each the strength of a thousand mothers

[*Mothers and Children together*]

O Mary Star of the Morning,
Our true Mother
Star of the Morning
Our dear Mother
Star of the Morning
We will give the world water to drink

Dell'interno

aria from Giancarlo Cazetti's L'anima di Marina

Sad, you are sad, say the pitying ones.
I have consulted my wisest friends,
I have brought my troubles to the priest,
I have knelt till my knees are cold.

But in no place does the sorrow part,
this curtain that muffles me from light and warmth.
I stare into green leaves but they do not open for me.
I sit in the sun and the sun stays cold.

It is as if the world itself has said No.
It offers to me only a cold surface, dull
but slick, where I cannot grasp hold.
It tells me this is the bed I have made.

Inland, I long for the sea. It too
is cold, but with time the cold goes warm
and its roar is like a mother's heart
and its No becomes the one I speak.

Sonnenwendenlieder
  (Solstice Songs)

Ungeliebt

So I offered a bargain:
All of it, the books, the papers,
and whatever is still brewing in my teapot head—

All of this, I said, I will surrender
if only I may have
the home that I have seen in his face.

The answer came at once: *No.*
What lies you tell, and call them love.

Weltgetummel

I cannot lose track of the world.

Not the sad carved face, Liebhaber und Leitbild,
who leant me into his arms,

weak with fear, when I knew the weakness
at last would let me,

the soft salt rising—
Not that. That's the other place.

So when I am jerked into this ticking world
I want to punish it, to break

the hard tumult of its fair questions,
its just demands, its not-that-ness.

Can you help, do you know,
where can I lie down, and what chuffing iron

will speed me to my longed-for loss.

Essen und Trinken

Love breaks me like a corn cake
in a boy's mouth.

I am eating my own heart but I would like to wash it first,
raccoon-like, in the Rhine.

I offered him our bloods' river to drown in
but he found the metaphor distasteful. When did I learn

to make fun of pain, my closed throat,
the disease of my longing that makes it impossible

even to suck the ice chips shoveled
between dry lips with a long-handled spoon?

No river would oblige, in any case,
on this continent or another.

Weiss Nacht

Red-gold hair spills through boar bristles,
and candles with their flames still lit lie down—
collars and buttons are talking, and cows
browse on the apples that will sour their milk.

Visions would be welcome but I am not visited so.

Tonight the usually warm shoulder of blackness
shrugged me off, it was cold milky glass.
And all this I deserved, since I who hate pain
will cause pain.

Romanze Krankheit

That last dose of laudanum would do it,
the beveled stopper caught
between exquisite fingers until they unfold.

It turns out childhood sweethearts don't remember.

The dead beloved has returned
in the body of a small jumping cat
who shies from my hand.

Anagrams and the gew-gaws of fortune-tellers are sought.

As advised, I threw his left shoe
into the river to take away our sorrow
but it has not worked.

Meanwhile the restraint between lovers writes its own syntax.

The fine delay of sand
drags each footstep
through cypress topiary.

Indirection is not the road out.

Letzt Ziga'rette, Letzt Kuss

O my friends, tonight the air
is too thick: Let's say
good-bye to our cigarettes

Let's unwrap them, crackle
and strew, gold virgin shreds
on a saucer: Bonfire

When your lover smiles
at another, ladies and gentlemen,
set your own smile on fire

And find a new lover, quick!
Or you will be smoking again,
I know you

A red bird flew into my mouth
and sang this song in flicks of flame:
Last cigarette, last kiss

Notes on the Poems

"To the Knife" is for Jason Shinder (1955–2008).

"Underneath" is for R.Q.F.

The novel and author referred to in "The Heroine in the Novel" are my own fictions.

The operas and composers referred to in the poems "Sonya to the Messenger," "Epithalamion," "Heimatlos," "Mary Star of the Morning," and "Dell'interno" are also fictional.

In "Sonnenwendenlieder (Solstice Songs)," the section titles mean "Unloved," "World Tumult," "Eating and Drinking," "White Night," and "Romance Sickness."

Acknowledgments

Grateful acknowledgement is made to the following publications, in which many of these poems first appeared: *Agni, A Public Space, Southwest Review, The Nation, The New Republic, The New York Review of Books, The New Yorker, Tight, Salmagundi.*

I am indebted to the Solomon Guggenheim Foundation for a grant that allowed me to work on these poems; to the Sidney Harman Foundation for support; and to the Corporation of Yaddo and The MacDowell Colony, both of which generously provided needed time and space.

I am indebted to my editor, Jill Bialosky, who has been patient and wise.

Finally, to those who generously listened and advised while I was writing these poems—especially Mark Conway, Annabel Davis-Goff, Alice Mattison, and Mark Wunderlich—I send my deepest thanks and love.